NATIONAL GEOGRAPHIC KiDS

PUZZLE BOOK

WHAT IN THE

WORLD

FACT-PACKED

FUN

CONTENTS

PUZZLE BOOK

WHAT IN THE

WORLD

FACT-PACKED

FUN

Published by Collins
An imprint of HarperCollins Publishers
Westerhill Road
Bishopbriggs
Glasgow G64 2QT
www.harpercollins.co.uk

In association with National Geographic Partners, LLC

NATIONAL GEOGRAPHIC and the Yellow Border Design are trademarks of the National Geographic Society, used under license.

First published 2018

ISBN 978-0-00-826773-5

10 9 8 7 6 5 4 3

A catalogue record for this book is available from the British Library

Printed and bound in China by RR Donnelley APS Co Ltd.

If you would like to comment on any aspect of this book,
please contact us at the above address or online.
natgeokidsbooks.co.uk
collins.reference@harpercollins.co.uk

Paper from responsible sources.

Acknowledgements

Cover images
Bald Eagle – Sekar B/Shutterstock.com; Accordion – Africa Studio/Shutterstock.com; Martial Arts–Happy Together/Shutterstock.com; Big Ben–antb/Shutterstock.com; Chichen Itza – Lukiyanova Natalia frenta/Shutterstock.com; Machu Picchu – Anton_Ivanov/Shutterstock.com; Football – Oleksii Sidorov/ Shutterstock.com; African Drum – Tatyana Vyc/ Shutterstock.com; Kangaroo – Eric Isselee/Shutterstock.com

Images in order of appearance
Taj Mahal–Nicole Kwiatkowski/Shutterstock.com; Koala–Eric Isselee / Shutterstock.com; British Guard – Boris-B Shutterstock.com; Croissant – Mindscape studio/ Shutterstock.com; Giraffe – a_v_d / Shutterstock.com; Panda–Eric Isselee/Shutterstock.com; Bald Eagle – Sekar B/ Shutterstock.com; Christ the Redeemer – R.M. Nunes/ Shutterstock.com; Koala–Eric Isselee/Shutterstock.com; World Map – Peter Hermes Furian / Shutterstock.com; Thistle – Le Do / Shutterstock.com; Fry-up plate – Richard M Lee/Shutterstock.com; Fish and chips–stocksolutions/Shutterstock.com; Strawberry–Maks Narodenko/Shutterstock.com; Leek – Peter Zijlstra / Shutterstock.com; Highland Cow–Chester Tugwell/Shutterstock.com; Deer–Mark Caunt/Shutterstock.com; Golf–Christopher Halloran/Shutterstock.com; Cricket – Rtimages/Shutterstock.com; Highland dancing scene – Paul McKinnon/ Shutterstock.com; Big Ben – antb/ Shutterstock.com; British Guard–Boris-B Shutterstock.com; Leaning Tower of Pisa – Be Good / Shutterstock.com; Croissant – Mindscape studio/ Shutterstock.com; Pizza – bestv/ Shutterstock.com; Paella – stockcreations/Shutterstock.com; Puffin–Eric Isselee/Shutterstock.com; Badger– charlie davidson/ Shutterstock.com; Flamenco–Andy-pix/ Shutterstock.com; Irish dancing – Lorraine Swanson/ Shutterstock.com; Accordion – Africa Studio/ Shutterstock.com; Skiing Alps scene – gorillaimages/ Shutterstock.com; Eiffel Tower – Roman Sigaev/ Shutterstock.com; Windmills – VanderWolf Images/ Shutterstock.com; Kilimanjaro – Volodymyr Burdiak / Shutterstock.com; Cassava – LAURA_VN/ Shutterstock.com; Coffee – Valentyn Volkov/Shutterstock.com; African Drum–Tatyana Vyc/Shutterstock.com; Tagine – nabil refaat / Shutterstock.com; Distance running – Maxisport / Shutterstock.com; Handball – Ana-Maria Tegzes / Shutterstock.com; Giraffe – Valdis Skudre/Shutterstock.com; Lion – FeraBG/ Shutterstock.com; Elephant – sevenke/ Shutterstock.com; Gorilla–Onyx9/Shutterstock.com; Camel – lovely pet/Shutterstock.com; Hippo – Redchanka/ Shutterstock.com; Pyramids – WitR/ Shutterstock.com; Sphinx – Paola Nerone/ Shutterstock.com; Taj Mahal – Nicole Kwiatkowski/Shutterstock.com; Sushi – Jag_cz/ Shutterstock.com; Dim Sum – Maffi/ Shutterstock.com; Tiger – KAMONRAT/ Shutterstock.com; Panda – Eric Isselee/ Shutterstock.com; Martial Arts – Happy Together/ Shutterstock.com; Cricket – AHMAD FAIZAL YAHYA / Shutterstock.com; Field Hockey – India Picture/Shutterstock.com; Thai market–karinkamon/Shutterstock.com; Burj Khalifa – Goran Bogicevic/ Shutterstock.com; Petronas Towers – saiko3p/ Shutterstock.com; Raccoon – Sonsedska Yuliia/ Shutterstock.com; Fried Chicken–dolphfyn/Shutterstock.com; Tacos – etorres/ Shutterstock.com; Brown bear – volkova natalia/ Shutterstock.com; Bald Eagle – Sekar B/ Shutterstock.com; Basketball–Chinaview/Shutterstock.com; Baseball–Andrey Yurlov/ Shutterstock.com; Ice Hockey – Andrey Yurlov/ Shutterstock.com; Havana – Stefanie Metzger / Shutterstock.com; Statue of Liberty – Luciano Mortula - LGM/Shutterstock.com; Chichen Itza – Lukiyanova Natalia frenta/Shutterstock.com; Toucan – Christopher Becerra/ Shutterstock.com; Empanadas – bonchan / Shutterstock.com; Picarones – Ildi Papp / Shutterstock.com; Alpaca – mariait/ Shutterstock.com; Tropical Frog–Peter Reijners/Shutterstock.com; Football – Oleksii Sidorov/ Shutterstock.com; Volleyball – Boris Ryaposov/Shutterstock.com; Beach Soccer– lazyllama/Shutterstock.com; Christ the Redeemer – R.M. Nunes/Shutterstock.com; Machu Picchu–Anton_Ivanov/Shutterstock.com; Surfing–Jorge Alejandro Russell/Shutterstock.com; Vegemite–PageSeven/Shutterstock.com; BBQ – Alexander Raths/Shutterstock.com; Kangaroo – Eric Isselee/ Shutterstock.com; Koala–Eric Isselee/Shutterstock.com; Emu–Anan Kaewkhammul / Shutterstock.com; Rugby – wavebreakmedia / Shutterstock.com; Aussie rules– Neale Cousland/Shutterstock.com; Sydney Opera House – Barbara185/ Shutterstock.com; Uluru – Stanislav Fosenbauer / Shutterstock.com; Boomerang – Richard Peterson/Shutterstock.com

WORLD MAP

NORTH AMERICA is **SITUATED** entirely in the the **NORTHERN** and **WESTERN HEMISPHERES.**

North America

SOUTH AMERICA has the **LONGEST MOUNTAIN RANGE** (the Andes) and the **HIGHEST WATERFALLS** (the Angel Falls).

South America

ANTARCTICA has **NO PERMANENT RESIDENTS** and **NO COUNTRIES.**

EUROPE is home to the **TWO SMALLEST COUNTRIES** in the world – **MONACO** and **THE VATICAN CITY**.

ASIA is the World's **LARGEST CONTINENT** and also the **MOST POPULATED**.

AUSTRALIA is one of the **LARGEST COUNTRIES** on Earth. **OVER ONE-THIRD** of Australia is **DESERT**.

AFRICA has the world's **LARGEST DESERT** (the Sahara), **LONGEST RIVER** (the Nile) and **MOST COUNTRIES** (54) of any continent.

Europe

Asia

Africa

Australia

Antarctica

United Kingdom

Uncover fun facts and puzzles on the United Kingdom over the next few pages.

THISTLES are **SCOTLAND'S NATIONAL FLOWER.** They are usually **PURPLE,** however, can bloom in a variety of colours including **WHITE** and **YELLOW.**

CROSSWORDS

Crack the crosswords by solving the cryptic clues below.
Answers have the same amount of letters as the number in brackets.
Can you work out the keywords from the United Kingdom using the letters in
the shaded squares? See if you are right by flicking to page 90.

More than **250 MILLION FISH** and **CHIP MEALS** are sold in the **UNITED KINGDOM** every **YEAR!**

Across
4 Very clever or talented (9)
6 Adult males (3)
8 Something to sit on (5)
9 Tube you can drink through (5)
10 A large primate (3)
12 Place in a school where lessons take place (9)

Down
1 Without cost or payment (4)
2 The direction the hands on a watch move (9)
3 Popular yellow fruit (6)
5 Number in a trio (5)
6 Melodic sounds (5)
7 Ordinary; regular (6)
11 Having very little money (4)

It is **TRADITIONAL** for Welsh people to wear leeks pinned to their **CLOTHES** or **HATS** on **ST DAVID'S DAY.**

Across

4 Someone might say 'bless you' if you do this (6)
6 Close by (4)
7 The sound of a contented cat (4)
8 Genuine (4)
9 Narrow road (4)
10 Type of spacecraft (6)

Down

1 Urge on (9)
2 Musical instrument (8)
3 Person in a story (9)
5 Way in (8)

SUDOKUS

Help the highland cow solve the sudokus. Fill in the blank squares so that numbers 1 to 6 appear once in each row, column and 3x2 box.
See if you are right by flicking to page 90.

A group of **COWS** is usually called a **'HERD'**, but a group of **HIGHLAND COWS** is called a **'FOLD'**.

5			2		
4	6		3		
6			4		
		4	1		5
		5		2	4
		6			

Top puzzle:

			3		
3			2	5	6
6					1
2					
1	6	5			2
		2			

Bottom puzzle:

1	2				5
				4	1
				6	
	3				
2	1				
4	5		1	2	6

Wordsearches

Get a hole in one by completing the wordsearches. Search left to right, up and down to find the words listed in the boxes below. See if you are right by flicking to page 90.

m	a	n	c	h	e	s	t	e	r
u	t	r	t	c	u	f	h	m	a
n	s	c	c	a	s	d	e	s	t
i	f	f	b	r	l	e	q	d	t
o	r	s	t	d	m	n	u	b	l
n	y	c	r	i	c	k	e	t	o
j	u	u	i	f	m	s	e	w	n
a	p	o	f	f	k	t	n	n	d
c	g	o	l	f	g	t	l	o	o
k	o	t	e	b	i	g	b	e	n

In **1457, GOLF** was banned by **KING JAMES II** of **SCOTLAND,** who said it was distracting **SOLDIERS** from practising archery.

Big Ben
Cardiff
cricket
fry-up
golf

London
Manchester
The Queen
trifle
Union Jack

Belfast
black cab
Edinburgh
leeks
Robin Hood

royalty
Stonehenge
tea and cake
Wimbledon
Windsor

One theory is that **CRICKET** may have been brought to the **UK** by **FLEMISH WEAVERS,** who used to play the game with their CROOKS **(SHEPHERDS' STICKS)** near their sheep.

s	t	o	n	e	h	e	n	g	e
j	w	i	n	d	s	o	r	v	a
l	o	b	l	a	c	k	c	a	b
u	s	b	e	l	f	a	s	t	s
w	i	m	b	l	e	d	o	n	l
r	o	y	a	l	t	y	o	i	e
t	e	a	a	n	d	c	a	k	e
l	f	l	p	e	f	g	d	q	k
e	d	i	n	b	u	r	g	h	s
s	r	o	b	i	n	h	o	o	d

SPOT THE DIFFERENCE

Compare the two images of the highland dancers.
Can you spot the five differences between the images?
See if you are right by flicking to page 91.

SCOTTISH HIGHLAND DANCING is very precise. In competitions dancers are judged on their **POSTURE, TECHNIQUE** and **TIMING.**

GUESS WHAT?

Can you guess the answers to the United Kingdom questions below?
Check your guesses by flicking to page 91.

1. What is traditionally consumed during afternoon tea?
   a) Tea, sandwiches and cakes
   b) Tea and burgers
   c) Tea and pizza

2. Which dessert dish contains sponge cake and fruit covered with layers of jelly, custard and cream?
   a) Mince pie
   b) Banoffee pie
   c) Trifle

3. What colour are London's famous buses?
   a) Blue
   b) Yellow
   c) Red

4. What is a fried breakfast also called?
   a) Fry-left
   b) Fry-up
   c) Fry-down

5. Which of these is a national emblem of Wales?
   a) Carrot
   b) Leek
   c) Parsnip

6. Which of these locations hosts a world-famous tennis tournament each year?
   a) Coventry
   b) Middlesex
   c) Wimbledon

7. What is the tallest building in the United Kingdom?
   a) The Gherkin
   b) The Shard
   c) Heron Tower

8. Where are the Crown Jewels kept?
   a) Windsor Castle
   b) The Tower of London
   c) The London Eye

9. Which of these is not an English football club?
   a) Chelsea
   b) Real Madrid
   c) Manchester United

10. What is the capital city of Wales?
    a) Wrexham
    b) Swansea
    c) Cardiff

Work your way around the maze until you reach the exit.
See if you are right by flicking to page 91.

MAZE

Word wheels

Can you work out the United Kingdom countries
in the two word wheels?
See if you are right by flicking to page 91.

Word wheel 1: N L A E D G N

Word wheel 2: A T C L N O S D

Europe

Enamoured by Europe? Explore this chapter for fun facts and puzzles.

It took nearly 200 YEARS to build the LEANING TOWER OF PISA.

CROSSWORDS

Grab a slice of pizza once you complete the crosswords by solving the cryptic clues below. Answers have the same amount of letters as the number in brackets. Can you work out the keywords from Europe using the letters in the shaded squares? See if you are right by flicking to page 92.

In **FRANCE, MOON-SHAPED** croissants are made with margarine, so they are **CHEAPER.** Straighter croissants are **BUTTERY** and more **EXPENSIVE.**

Across
1. Tenth month of the year (7)
6. Approve or suggest someone or something (9)
8. Yellow vegetable (9)
9. Serving no purpose (7)

Down
2. Green vegetables (9)
3. People vote for politicians in these (9)
4. E.g. from Wales or England (7)
5. Loving dearly (7)
7. Slightly wet (5)

TRADITIONAL PAELLA was first made by **SPANISH RICE FARMERS** and only included **INGREDIENTS** that could be found in the nearby fields.

Across

4 Very well-known (6)
6 Sort (4)
7 You hear with this (3)
8 Fierce sound of a lion (4)
9 What you see with (4)
10 Machine that blows cool air (3)
11 List of food items at a restaurant (4)
12 Note (6)

Down

1 Trick-or-treating happens on this day (9)
2 Very strong (8)
3 Ninth month (9)
5 Might; power (8)

SUDOKUS

Help the puffin solve the sudokus. Fill in the blank squares so that numbers 1 to 6 appear once in each row, column and 3x2 box. See if you are right by flicking to page 9?

5	6	1			4
		3			
	1		4		
4	5	6		2	
			5		
			1	4	3

PUFFINS can't take off easily from the **GROUND** – in order to fly, they have a running start or jump off **CLIFFS** and then **FLAP, FLAP, FLAP!**

The **BADGER** is said to get its name from the **FRENCH** word **'BECHEUR'**, which means **'DIGGER'**.

Wordsearches

Search the dancefloor left to right, up and down to find the words listed in the boxes below.
See if you are right by flicking to page 92.

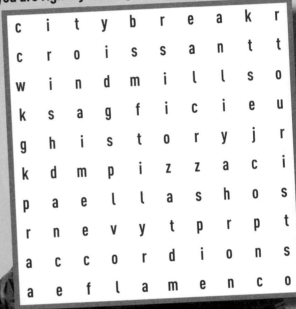

c	i	t	y	b	r	e	a	k	r
c	r	o	i	s	s	a	n	t	t
w	i	n	d	m	i	l	l	s	o
k	s	a	g	f	i	c	i	e	u
g	h	i	s	t	o	r	y	j	r
k	d	m	p	i	z	z	a	c	i
p	a	e	l	l	a	s	h	o	s
r	n	e	v	y	t	p	r	p	t
a	c	c	o	r	d	i	o	n	s
a	e	f	l	a	m	e	n	c	o

SPANISH FLAMENCO DANCING traditionally combines dancing with singing, playing guitar, **CLAPPING, FOOT STOMPING,** and **SHOUTING.**

accordion

city break

croissant

flamenco

history

Irish dance

paella

pizza

tourists

windmills

26

g	i	p	z	c	p	c	r	t	k
a	a	o	e	z	h	j	m	s	i
c	j	e	g	r	e	e	c	e	r
a	g	v	o	e	a	t	g	n	e
s	c	f	r	a	n	c	e	g	l
p	l	u	a	p	r	l	r	l	a
a	y	w	a	l	e	s	m	a	n
i	x	s	c	o	t	l	a	n	d
n	s	s	w	e	d	e	n	d	r
z	l	o	i	t	a	l	y	e	r

England
France
Germany
Greece
Ireland

Italy
Scotland
Spain
Sweden
Wales

ACCORDIONS are sometimes called **'SQUEEZE BOXES'** because of the way they are played.

SPOT THE DIFFERENCE

Compare the two images of the skiers.
Can you spot the five differences between the images?
See if you are right by flicking to page 93.

See if you are right by flicking to page 93.

The **ALPS** are the biggest **MOUNTAIN** range in **EUROPE**, stretching across eight different countries, and are a very popular place to go **SKIING.**

GUESS WHAT?

Can you guess the answers to the Europe questions below?
Check your guesses by flicking to page 93.

1. Where is Italy's famous leaning tower?
   a) Palermo
   b) Pisa
   c) Pompeii

2. Which European country is famous for windmills?
   a) Estonia
   b) Latvia
   c) The Netherlands

3. Which tower would you climb in Paris?
   a) Petronas
   b) Louvre
   c) Eiffel

4. Which of these is a traditional Spanish meal?
   a) Goulash
   b) Paella
   c) Pizza

5. Which of these is a French pastry?
   a) Bagel
   b) Croissant
   c) Strudel

6. Where are you most likely to take in the opera?
   a) Vienna
   b) Oslo
   c) Dublin

7. Slovenia's famous lake is called?
   a) Lake Thames
   b) Lake Bled
   c) Lake Rhein

8. Where is Flamenco dancing popular?
   a) Serbia
   b) Spain
   c) Slovakia

9. Where are the popular European ski slopes?
   a) The Alps
   b) The Andes
   c) The Himalayas

10. Which country is not a Baltic state?
    a) Denmark
    b) Estonia
    c) Lithuania

MAZE

Work your way around the maze until you reach the exit. See if you are right by flicking to page 93.

Word wheels

Can you work out the European countries in the two word wheels?
See if you are right by flicking to page 93.

Africa

Amazed by Africa? Read on for fun facts and puzzles on this vast continent.

MOUNT KILIMANJARO in **TANZANIA** towers at **5,895 METRES** tall. It is the **LARGEST FREESTANDING MOUNTAIN** in the **WORLD.**

CROSSWORDS

Fill in the crosswords by solving the cryptic clues below.
Answers have the same amount of letters as the number in brackets.
Can you work out the keywords from Africa using the letters in the shaded squares?
See if you are right by flicking to page 94.

CASSAVA is also known as **TAPIOCA, YUCCA,** and **MANIOC** – it is one of the most important crops in **AFRICA.**

Across

1. Trustworthy (8)
5. Block of chocolate; prevent (3)
6. Districts or regions (5)
7. Short curved hairs that grow on part of your face (9)
10. Very simple (5)
11. A colour on traffic lights (3)
12. Seriously or harshly (8)

Down

2. Big (5)
3. Mass of snow or rock sliding down a mountain (9)
4. Escape or avoid (5)
8. E.g. 2018 and 2019 (5)
9. Animal that is ridden by jockeys (5)

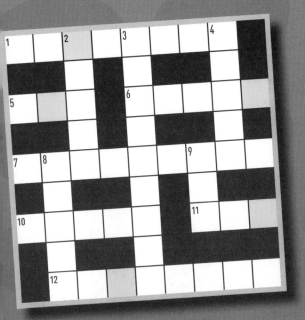

It's said that an **ETHIOPIAN GOAT** herder discovered **COFFEE** after noticing that his goats ate certain berries and became too energetic to **SLEEP**.

Across

1. Green vegetable eaten in salads (8)
5. Not near (3)
6. Appears (5)
7. Person who might catch cod (9)
10. Famous cartoon deer (5)
11. Dirt (3)
12. Continual (8)

Down

2. There are 52 of these in a standard pack (5)
3. Unexplained things (9)
4. Type of dance (5)
8. ___ Newton: scientist who discovered gravity (5)
9. Opposite of dad (3)

SUDOKUS

Bang the drum when you solve the sudokus. Fill in the blank squares so that numbers 1 to 6 appear once in each row, column and 3x2 box.
See if you are right by flicking to page 94.

AFRICAN drums have been used for music, communication, celebration, and religious **FESTIVALS** for around **700 YEARS!**

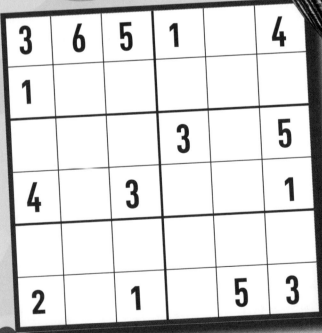

3	6	5	1		4
1					
			3		5
4		3			1
2		1		5	3

Top puzzle

					5
6	5		3		4
4			2		
		2			1
	2	3		5	6
5					2

Bottom puzzle

			1	5	
5				3	6
		2			
1			3		2
4	3				5
	6	5			3

Wordsearches

Hit the road and keep your eyes peeled for the African terms.
Search left to right, up and down to find the words listed in the boxes below.
See if you are right by flicking to page 94.

c	p	y	r	a	m	i	d	s	r
o	r	m	a	v	d	u	b	h	k
f	b	c	i	a	e	r	r	s	p
f	t	a	n	s	s	j	d	a	h
e	w	s	f	a	e	s	u	v	y
e	s	s	o	f	r	p	a	a	e
w	m	a	r	a	t	h	o	n	n
i	e	v	e	r	p	i	a	n	a
c	l	a	s	i	o	n	p	a	x
f	h	s	t	a	y	x	s	y	p

cassava	pyramids
coffee	rainforest
desert	safari
hyena	savanna
marathon	sphinx

f	n	d	y	o	p	p	p	s	s
l	a	g	l	t	g	a	n	t	n
z	m	o	g	h	a	n	a	u	t
o	o	k	e	y	z	i	f	n	u
e	r	e	o	e	e	l	a	i	r
i	o	n	t	n	l	e	r	s	o
i	c	y	j	a	l	z	m	i	p
p	c	a	l	g	e	r	i	a	r
m	o	u	n	t	a	i	n	s	n
l	l	x	o	z	a	e	g	z	m

ETHIOPIAN Haile Gebrselassie was one of the **GREATEST DISTANCE RUNNERS** in the world, winning the Berlin marathon 4 times in a row and breaking the **WORLD MARATHON RECORD** twice!

The **AFRICAN HANDBALL NATIONS CHAMPIONSHIP** is the oldest continental handball competition. **TUNISIA** have won it **NINE TIMES** – more wins than any other nation!

Algeria
farming
gazelle
Ghana
Guinea

Kenya
Morocco
mountains
Nile
Tunisia

CLOSE UP

Match the mind-boggling magnifications to the named pictures opposite. See if you are right by flicking to page 95.

1 Hippo

2 Gorilla

3 Lion

4 Giraffe

5 Elephant

6 Camel

41

GUESS WHAT?

Can you guess the answers to the Africa questions below?
Check your guesses by flicking to page 95.

1. Which of these is a South African fast food dish?
   a) Sheep chow
   b) Cow chow
   c) Bunny chow

2. Which of these is the longest river in Africa?
   a) River Nile
   b) River File
   c) River Mile

3. Which of these is a desert in Africa?
   a) Sarah
   b) Sahara
   c) Savannah

4. Which of these countries is furthest North?
   a) Chad
   b) Morocco
   c) Angola

5. Which currency is used in Ghana?
   a) Pound
   b) Dollar
   c) Cedi

6. Which of these cities is in Egypt?
   a) Cairo
   b) Lagos
   c) Johannesburg

7. Which is the largest city on the African continent?
   a) Casablanca
   b) Abuja
   c) Lagos

8. Which is the only continent bigger than Africa?
   a) Asia
   b) Europe
   c) Australia

9. If you visited Nairobi, where would you be?
   a) Tunisia
   b) Kenya
   c) Libya

10. Which name is given to a trip to observe animals, especially in Africa?
    a) Safari
    b) Voyage
    c) Marathon

Work your way around the maze
until you reach the exit.
See if you are right by flicking to
page 95.

Word wheels

Can you work out the African countries
in the two word wheels?
See if you are right by flicking to page 95.

Asia

Your Asian adventure starts here. Explore this chapter for fun facts and puzzles on the world's largest continent.

It took around **20,000** workers, and over **1,000 ELEPHANTS**, to build the **TAJ MAHAL MAUSOLEUM.**

CROSSWORDS

Enjoy some sushi once you crack the crosswords by solving the cryptic clues below.
Answers have the same amount of letters as the number in brackets.
Can you work out the keywords from Asia using the letters in the shaded squares?
See if you are right by flicking to page 96.

Across

1 Tragedy (8)
5 Insect that makes honey (3)
6 Opposite of west (5)
7 Neil ___ : first person to walk on the moon (9)
10 Sad or unhappy (5)
11 Snake-like fish (3)
12 Become less (8)

Down

2 Water vapour (5)
3 Person who watches an event (9)
4 A type of rodent (3)
8 Swift (5)
9 Musical drama (5)

Back in the **8TH CENTURY, SUSHI** was so special that some **JAPANESE** people could use it to pay their **TAXES!**

CHINESE DIM SUM are **BITE-SIZED** portions of various foods, traditionally served in special **STEAMER BASKETS** and with **TEA.**

Across
1 Hurt hog (anagram) (7)
6 Constant; lasting indefinitely (9)
8 Change the order of items (9)
9 Opposite of strongest (7)

Down
2 Major storm (9)
3 Words of welcome (9)
4 Eight-legged creatures (7)
5 Where horses are kept (7)
7 Film or TV performer (5)

SUDOKUS

Help the tiger complete the sudokus. Fill in the blank squares so that numbers 1 to 6 appear once in each row, column and 3x2 box.
See if you are right by flicking to page 96.

Fossils found in **CHINA** show that **TIGERS** have walked the **EARTH** for around **2 MILLION YEARS!**

1	5		2		6
				5	
		1	5		
		6	1		
	6				1
3		4		2	

4	3	2			1
	6				4
				2	6
2	1				
3				1	
6			3		2

The **SCIENTIFIC** name for a **GIANT PANDA** is *Ailuropoda melanoleuca*, which means '**BLACK** and **WHITE CAT-FOOT**'.

2	6	1			
	4	5	6	3	
		6	5	4	
		4	2	6	3

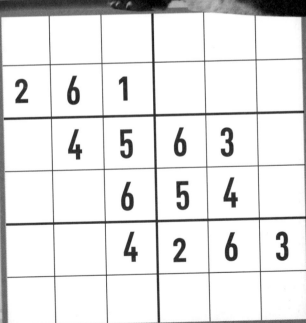

Wordsearches

Complete the wordsearches to receive your black belt.
Search left to right, up and down to find the words listed in the boxes below.
See if you are right by flicking to page 96.

s	y	g	a	k	c	h	i	n	a
h	x	o	o	u	r	f	s	u	r
i	i	b	i	l	i	w	s	p	j
m	k	i	n	g	c	o	b	r	a
a	s	d	d	y	k	s	b	f	p
l	a	e	i	s	e	r	n	t	a
a	h	s	a	l	t	t	d	u	n
y	b	e	n	g	a	l	f	o	x
a	g	r	e	a	t	w	a	l	l
s	s	t	f	p	a	n	d	a	l

The **INDIAN HOCKEY** team was one of the very first **INDIAN SPORTS** teams to go on a round-the-**WORLD TOUR.**

Bengal fox
China
cricket
Gobi Desert
Great Wall

Himalayas
India
Japan
king cobra
panda

```
g  g  b  a  m  b  o  o  w  g
r  t  p  a  k  i  s  t  a  n
a  x  e  w  s  u  a  u  s  a
s  o  u  t  h  k  o  r  e  a
s  t  h  o  n  g  k  o  n  g
l  t  h  a  i  l  a  n  d  s
a  p  q  j  u  d  o  n  v  i
n  s  e  z  o  r  e  l  m  l
d  r  t  i  g  e  r  t  o  k
s  i  n  g  a  p  o  r  e  m
```

'KARATE' is a Japanese word meaning 'empty hand'. Karate is less about fighting, and more about the art of **SELF-DEFENCE.**

bamboo
grasslands
Hong Kong
judo
Pakistan

silk
Singapore
South Korea
Thailand
tiger

Compare the two images of the floating market in Thailand.
Can you spot the five differences between the images?
See if you are right by flicking to page 97.

See if you are right by flicking to page 97.

FLOATING MARKETS have existed for centuries and are found mainly in **THAILAND, INDONESIA** and **VIETNAM.**

GUESS WHAT?

Can you guess the answers to the Asia questions below?
Check your guesses by flicking to page 97.

1. What is the approximate population of Asia?
   a) 4.5 trillion
   b) 4.5 billion
   c) 4.5 million

2. Which of these is the capital city of India?
   a) Chennai
   b) Pune
   c) New Delhi

3. Which of these colours is found on the flag of Pakistan?
   a) Yellow
   b) Green
   c) Red

4. Which of these is an Asian dish?
   a) Chicken satay
   b) Fish and chips
   c) Pizza

5. Which of these Asian mountains is the tallest in the world?
   a) Mount Everest
   b) Mount Tahan
   c) Mount Hua

6. Which Indonesian island is the world's most populous island?
   a) Guava
   b) Lava
   c) Java

7. Which of these is in Asia?
   a) The Great Wall of China
   b) Hollywood sign
   c) Notre Dame

8. What colours are found on the Japanese flag?
   a) Black and blue
   b) Red and white
   c) Yellow and red

9. Which of these cities is found in Japan?
   a) Athens
   b) Tokyo
   c) Lisbon

10. What is the capital city of Thailand?
    a) Bangkok
    b) Beijing
    c) New Delhi

MAZE

Work your way around the maze until you reach the exit. See if you are right by flicking to page 97.

See if you are right by flicking to page 97.

The **BURJ KHALIFA** in **DUBAI, U.A.E** is the **WORLD'S TALLEST BUILDING,** measuring over **828 METRES** tall!

Word wheels

Can you work out the Asian countries in the two word wheels?
See if you are right by flicking to page 97.

See if you are right by flicking to page 97.

I A
H
C N

A Y
A L
M
A S
I

55

North America

Read on for fun facts and puzzles on North America.

RACCOONS have very sensitive **FRONT PAWS,** which become extra **SENSITIVE** when they use **TOUCH** to explore objects **UNDERWATER.**

CROSSWORDS

Feast on some fried chicken once you complete the crosswords by solving the cryptic clues below. Answers have the same amount of letters as the number in brackets. Can you work out the keywords from North America using the letters in the shaded squares? See if you are right by flicking to page 98.

Before **WORLD WAR II,** fried chicken was expensive and only **EATEN** on special occasions – now it's one of the most consumed fast **FOODS!**

Across

4 Hard (9)
6 One plus one (3)
8 Go into a room (5)
9 Form of public transport on rails (5)
10 Finish (3)
12 Bright flash that is followed by thunder (9)

Down

1 Outlook; field of vision (4)
2 Go to sleep through the winter (9)
3 Animal that looks like a tortoise (6)
5 Weary (5)
6 Sum (5)
7 Colour; citrus fruit (6)
11 Zero (4)

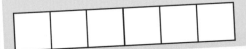

Across

4 Quantity (6)
6 Turn over and over (4)
7 Item of neckwear often worn with a suit (3)
8 Thought or suggestion (4)
9 Additionally (4)
10 Form of public transport (3)
11 Hard part at the end of a finger (4)
12 Continent (6)

Down

1 Instant (9)
2 Appropriate (8)
3 Device used to study stars (9)
5 Jewels and other valuable items (8)

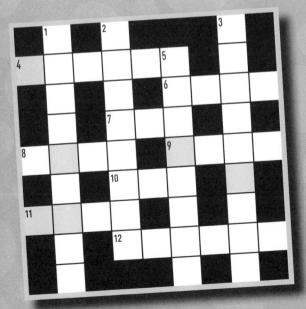

On National Taco Day, which is celebrated in **OCTOBER,** North **AMERICANS** eat around **4.5 BILLION TACOS!**

SUDOKUS

Help the bald eagle solve the sudokus. Fill in the blank squares so that numbers 1 to 6 appear once in each row, column and 3x2 box. See if you are right by flicking to page 98.

BALD EAGLES have great eyesight and can still see even when they **BLINK** thanks to special translucent inner **EYELIDS.**

3	6			2		4
					1	
	2			1		
		5			6	
	4					
5	1	2		6		3

Top puzzle

5		2		6	1
1		6	3		
	5				4
2				3	
		5			3
	6		2		

Bottom puzzle

5	6				
4				6	3
1	4				
3				4	5
2	3				1
				2	4

Brown **BEARS** love to eat moths – a **LARGE MALE** can eat up to **40,000** in one day!

Wordsearches

Complete the wordsearches to hit a home run. Search left to right, up and down to find the words listed in the boxes below. See if you are right by flicking to page 98.

s	g	r	w	b	t	b	l	m	s
z	c	a	n	a	d	a	i	e	k
b	n	c	b	s	s	l	c	x	y
v	e	n	a	k	t	d	e	i	s
e	w	t	s	e	r	e	h	c	c
s	y	o	e	t	g	a	o	o	r
a	o	w	b	b	f	g	c	y	a
r	r	e	a	a	s	l	k	o	p
s	k	r	l	l	l	e	e	t	e
x	s	s	l	l	i	n	y	e	r

ICE HOCKEY is the most popular sport in **CANADA** and is thought to have been invented by the British, brought to Canada by immigrants and soldiers.

bald eagle

baseball

basketball

Canada

CN Tower

coyote

ice hockey

Mexico

New York

skyscraper

```
l a k e h u r o n l
h o l l y w o o d o
c h i c a g o l p s
p i m f l o r i d a
t o r o n t o y f n
o r u a t n l i u g
a i t s e a t t l e
k v v d t k s v d l
k e y l i m e p i e
y r u a s t e x a s
```

Chicago
Florida
Hollywood
key lime pie
Lake Huron

Los Angeles
Ohio River
Seattle
Texas
Toronto

SPOT THE DIFFERENCE

Compare the two images of Havana, Cuba.
Can you spot the five differences between the images?
See if you are right by flicking to page 99.

CUBA is the **LARGEST ISLAND** in the **CARIBBEAN SEA,** measuring **1,200 KM** from east to west.

GUESS WHAT?

Can you guess the answers to the North America questions below?
Check your guesses by flicking to page 99.

1. What are the main languages of North America?
   a) Welsh, French and English
   b) English, Spanish and French
   c) Russian, German and Spanish

2. What is the capital city of the United States?
   a) Washington, D.C.
   b) Chicago
   c) Los Angeles

3. Where is the CN Tower?
   a) Texas
   b) Toronto
   c) Florida

4. The flag of which country contains a maple leaf?
   a) Mexico
   b) Canada
   c) Cuba

5. Which of these colours does not appear on the Jamaican flag?
   a) Purple
   b) Green
   c) Yellow

6. Which of these desserts is from America?
   a) Bakewell tart
   b) Key lime pie
   c) Baklava

7. What is sourdough a type of?
   a) Sweet
   b) Bread
   c) Chicken

8. What is the name of the currency of Mexico?
   a) Yen
   b) Peso
   c) Pound

9. What is the capital city of Canada?
   a) Toronto
   b) Kingston
   c) Ottawa

10. Where is the famous Hollywood sign found?
    a) California
    b) Jamaica
    c) Mexico

M A Z E

EL CASTILLO is a famous PYRAMID in the Mexican archaelogical site of CHICHEN ITZA.

Work your way around the maze until you reach the exit. See if you are right by flicking to page 99.

Word wheels

Can you work out the North American countries in the two word wheels? See if you are right by flicking to page 99.

South America

Delve into the next chapter for fun facts and puzzles on splendid South America.

TOUCANS' BEAKS are very **LARGE** but, because they are made out of **HONEYCOMB KERATIN**, they are not very **HEAVY**.

CROSSWORDS

Treat yourself to some empanadas when you complete the crosswords by solving the cryptic clues below. Answers have the same amount of letters as the number in brackets. Can you work out the keywords from South America using the letters in the shaded squares? See if you are right by flicking to page 100.

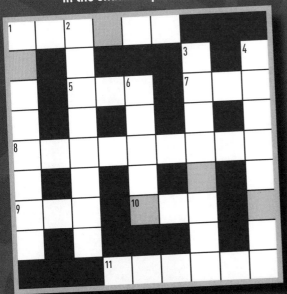

EMPANADAS are little **SOUTH AMERICAN PASTRIES** that come with a variety of fillings such as beef and cheese.

Across

1. Number in a dozen (6)
5. Obtained (3)
7. Foot extremity (3)
8. Person who goes into space (9)
9. Organ you see with (3)
10. Cuddle (3)
11. Middle (6)

Down

1. Person aged 13–19 (8)
2. Two times nine (8)
3. Without any bends; direct (8)
4. Octopus part (8)
6. When this falls out a fairy might visit you (5)

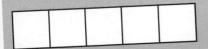

PICARONES are **PERUVIAN DOUGHNUTS** often sold as street food. They get their orange colour from the **SWEET POTATO/PUMPKIN** they are made from.

Across

1. Move from place to place; make a journey (6)
5. Opposite of no (3)
7. Sprint (3)
8. We sit hero (anagram) (9)
9. This star provides us with heat and light (3)
10. Small green vegetable (3)
11. Turn to ice (6)

Down

1. Animal with a hard shell (8)
2. Nay night (anagram) (8)
3. Annoy (8)
4. You put a letter in this before posting it (8)
6. Sweet and sticky liquid (5)

SUDOKUS

Help the alpaca solve the sudokus. Fill in the blank squares so that numbers 1 to 6 appear once in each row, column and 3x2 box.
See if you are right by flicking to page 100.

There are two main types of **ALPACA**: the **SURI** has long, **SILKY LOCKS,** and the **HUACAYA** has fluffy wool like a **TEDDY BEAR.**

3				5	1
	5				4
		2			3
4			1		6
5				3	
6	2				5

Puzzle 1 (6×6):

		1	6		
3					2
1			2		3
5		2			4
2					
6	4	5	3		

Puzzle 2 (6×6):

6		3		1	5
5	1			3	
		2			
			6		
	3			6	
1	4		5		3

Wordsearches

Hit the back of the net when you complete the wordsearches.
Search left to right, up and down to find the words listed in the boxes below.
See if you are right by flicking to page 100.

c	k	s	p	s	w	c	p	l	a
a	m	a	c	a	w	h	i	b	t
r	i	m	l	o	t	o	s	r	i
n	a	b	i	p	m	c	o	a	s
i	u	a	m	a	z	o	n	z	s
v	r	a	a	u	u	l	g	i	r
a	n	g	e	l	f	a	l	l	s
l	u	t	x	o	t	t	q	s	y
s	m	c	o	f	f	e	e	b	a
u	u	e	a	y	t	n	h	a	v

FOOTBALL is the most played sport and the most popular hobby in the whole of **SOUTH AMERICA**; it is especially loved in **BRAZIL**.

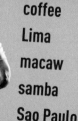

Amazon
Angel Falls
Brazil
carnivals
chocolate

coffee
Lima
macaw
samba
Sao Paulo

```
m  v  u  v  a  o  b  e  e  t
z  p  r  e  c  p  o  q  c  u
j  i  u  n  o  e  l  n  u  v
a  r  g  e  n  t  i  n  a  f
g  a  u  z  c  p  v  t  d  t
u  n  a  u  a  e  i  g  o  u
a  h  y  e  g  r  a  j  r  r
r  a  p  l  u  u  w  t  l  f
d  s  t  a  a  c  h  i  l  e
s  o  o  t  h  c  g  a  q  p
```

Aconcagua
Argentina
Bolivia
Chile
Ecuador
jaguar
Peru
piranhas
Uruguay
Venezuela

Compare the two images of the beach football players.
Can you spot the five differences between the images?
See if you are right by flicking to page 101.

See if you are right by flicking to page 101.

The first professional
BEACH FOOTBALL
competition was held
in **1993** at **MIAMI
BEACH, FLORIDA.**

GUESS WHAT?

Can you guess the answers to the South America questions below?
Check your guesses by flicking to page 101.

1. What is the famous mountain in Rio de Janeiro?
   a) Pepper Loaf Mountain
   b) Sugar Loaf Mountain
   c) Salt Loaf Mountain

2. Where would you find Machu Picchu?
   a) Peru
   b) Colombia
   c) Paraguay

3. Where is the Atacama Desert?
   a) Argentina
   b) Brazil
   c) Chile

4. What meat is Argentina famous for farming?
   a) Pork
   b) Beef
   c) Lamb

5. Asunción is the capital city of which country?
   a) Uruguay
   b) Paraguay
   c) Venezuela

6. Which colours make up the Colombian flag?
   a) Yellow, blue and red
   b) Red, white and blue
   c) Red, yellow and green

7. Which river flows through South America?
   a) Nile
   b) Thames
   c) Amazon

8. The highest mountain in South America is:
   a) Aconcagua
   b) Everest
   c) Matterhorn

9. The smallest country in South America is:
   a) Guyana
   b) Ecuador
   c) Suriname

10. The language mainly spoken in Brazil is:
    a) Portuguese
    b) Spanish
    c) Brazilian

MAZE

Work your way around the maze until you reach the exit. See if you are right by flicking to page 101.

Word wheels

Can you work out the South American countries in the two word wheels?
See if you are right by flicking to page 101.

Oceania

Dive into the next chapter for
fun facts and puzzles
on awesome
Oceania.

SURFERS spend most
of their **TIME** waiting
or **PADDLING,** and
only 8 % of their **TIME**
surfing **WAVES!**

CROSSWORDS

Celebrate with a barbecue when you complete the crosswords by solving the cryptic clues below. Answers have the same amount of letters as the number in brackets. Can you work out the keywords from Oceania using the letters in the shaded squares? See if you are right by flicking to page 102.

BARBECUES are a big part of **AUSTRALIAN** culture – some **AUSTRALIANS** even have a barbecue on **CHRISTMAS DAY!**

Across
1. Large cats with striped coats (6)
6. E.g. Chess or backgammon (5,4)
7. Present (4)
8. Opposite of front (4)
9. Notice taken of something (9)
11. Spiritual beings (6)

Down
1. Sledge (8)
2. Text or images scribbled onto walls (8)
3. Thin pole used by fishermen (3)
4. Publication bought at a newsagent (8)
5. Saturdays and Sundays collectively (8)
10. Member of a religious community of women (3)

VEGEMITE is a salty **AUSTRALIAN** paste made from the yeast that is left over after brewing **BEER.**

Across
1. Network of train tracks (7)
6. Perfect (5)
7. Tennis tournament played on grass (9)
8. Comic featuring Dennis the Menace (5)
9. Leo ___ : famous Russian author (7)

Down
1. ___ energy: energy that will never run out (9)
2. Quickly spinning mass of water (9)
3. Gave in to; eyed lid (anagram) (7)
4. Optional (9)
5. Flexible athlete (7)

SUDOKUS

Help the koala solve the sudokus. Fill in the blank squares so that numbers 1 to 6 appear once in each row, column and 3x2 box.
See if you are right by flicking to page 102.

When a **BABY KANGAROO** is **BORN**, it's about the size of a **GRAPE** and has no fur at all!

	1	2	5	6	4
		5			1
6			1		
		1			6
2			4		5
1	5			2	

EMUS are too big to fly, but they can run at up to **30 MILES PER HOUR** and are great **SWIMMERS** too!

Wordsearches

Score a try when you complete the wordsearches. Search left to right, up and down to find the words listed in the boxes below. See if you are right by flicking to page 102.

NEW ZEALAND'S national **RUGBY TEAM,** the **ALL BLACKS,** start every game with an intimidating **MAORI** war dance called **'THE HAKA'.**

k	a	u	s	t	r	a	l	i	a
a	l	r	o	h	s	r	e	k	v
n	e	w	z	e	a	l	a	n	d
g	a	x	f	o	r	t	a	s	x
a	w	p	s	u	r	f	i	n	g
r	p	e	r	t	h	e	d	a	r
o	w	o	m	b	a	t	i	r	f
o	p	e	r	a	h	o	u	s	e
r	q	p	a	c	i	f	i	c	h
i	p	e	l	k	o	a	l	a	i

Australia
kangaroo
koala
New Zealand
Opera House
Pacific
Perth
surfing
The Outback
wombat

AUSTRALIAN FOOTBALL is quite similar to **RUGBY,** but one big difference is that it's played on an **OVAL-SHAPED PITCH,** not a rectangular one.

a	w	b	a	r	b	e	c	u	e
v	e	g	e	m	i	t	e	g	a
s	l	a	d	e	l	a	i	d	e
y	l	w	w	a	l	l	a	b	y
d	i	d	g	e	r	i	d	o	o
n	n	c	a	n	b	e	r	r	a
e	g	o	l	d	c	o	a	s	t
y	t	r	n	y	s	r	i	p	k
b	o	n	d	i	b	e	a	c	h
s	n	r	w	h	s	r	s	w	n

Adelaide
barbecue
Bondi Beach
Canberra
didgeridoo
Gold Coast
Sydney
vegemite
wallaby
Wellington

GUESS WHAT?

Can you guess the answers to the Oceania questions below?
Check your guesses by flicking to page 103.

1. Which of these is an informal name for Australia?
   a) Up over
   b) Down under
   c) Under over

2. Which of these is a famous resort region on the east coast of Australia?
   a) Gold Coast
   b) Silver Coast
   c) Bronze Coast

3. What name is given to New Zealand's famous rugby team?
   a) All Whites
   b) All Reds
   c) All Blacks

4. What might you eat at a barbecue?
   a) Burgers
   b) Roast dinner
   c) Spaghetti bolognese

5. Which of these is a famous landmark in Sydney?
   a) Sydney Theatre House
   b) Sydney Opera House
   c) Sydney Cinema House

6. The leaves of which tree make up most of the diet of a koala?
   a) Maple
   b) Oak
   c) Eucalyptus

7. Where is Bondi Beach?
   a) New Zealand
   b) Australia
   c) Fiji

8. Which animal is known for jumping?
   a) Kangaroo
   b) Koala
   c) Platypus

9. What is Uluru?
   a) A massive sandstone rock
   b) A traditional dance
   c) A traditional food

10. What is a didgeridoo?
   a) A sea creature
   b) A type of surfboard
   c) A wind instrument

MAZE

Work your way around the maze until you reach the exit.
See if you are right by flicking to page 103.

Word wheels

Can you work out the Oceania countries
in the two word wheels?
See if you are right by flicking to page 103.

Solutions

Crosswords

Crossword 1:
```
  F     C   B
B R I L L I A N T
  E     O   N   H
M E N   C H A I R
U   O   K   N   E
S T R A W   A P E
I   M   I   O
C L A S S R O O M
    L       R
```
Keyword: WALES

Crossword 2:
```
    E   R       C
S N E E Z E     H
    C   C   N E A R
    O   O   T   R
P U R R     R E A L
    R   D   A   C
L A N E     N   T
    G   R O C K E T
    E       E   R
```
Keyword: LONDON

Sudokus

5	1	3	2	4	6
4	6	2	3	5	1
6	5	1	4	3	2
3	2	4	1	6	5
1	3	5	6	2	4
2	4	6	5	1	3

5	2	6	3	1	4
3	1	4	2	5	6
6	4	3	5	2	1
2	5	1	6	4	3
1	6	5	4	3	2
4	3	2	1	6	5

1	2	4	6	3	5
3	6	5	2	4	1
5	4	1	3	6	2
6	3	2	5	1	4
2	1	6	4	5	3
4	5	3	1	2	6

Wordsearches

```
m a n c h e s t e r
u t r t c u f h m a
n s c c a s d e s t
i f f b r l e q d t
o r s t d m n u b l
n y c r i c k e t o
j u u i f m s e w n
a p o f f k t n n d
c g o l f g t l o o
k o t e b i g b e n
```

```
s t o n e h e n g e
j w i n d s o r v a
l o b l a c k c a b
u s b e l f a s t s
w i m b l e d o n l
r o y a l t y o i e
t e a a n d c a k e
l f l p e f g d q k
e d i n b u r g h s
s r o b i n h o o d
```

Spot the difference

Page 16–17

Page 18–19

Guess what?

1) a – Tea, sandwiches and cakes
2) c – Trifle
3) c – Red
4) b – Fry-up
5) b – Leek
6) c – Wimbledon
7) b – The Shard
8) b – The Tower of London
9) b – Real Madrid
10) c – Cardiff

Maze

Word wheels

England, Scotland

Solutions

Page 22-23

Crosswords

```
  O C T O B E R     R
B U       L       A
R E C O M M E N D
I   U       O     O
T   M       I     R
I   B       S     I
S W E E T C O R N
H   R       N     G
  U S E L E S S
```
Keyword: SWEDEN

```
    H   P             S
F A M O U S   S E
    L   W     T Y P E
    L   E A R   T
R O A R     E Y E S
    W   F A N     M
M E N U     G     B
E     L E T T E R
N           H     R
```
Keyword: NORWAY

Page 24-25

Sudokus

5	6	1	2	3	4
2	4	3	6	1	5
3	1	2	4	5	6
4	5	6	3	2	1
1	3	4	5	6	2
6	2	5	1	4	3

3	5	1	2	4	6
2	6	4	3	1	5
4	3	5	1	6	2
6	1	2	4	5	3
5	4	3	6	2	1
1	2	6	5	3	4

4	2	6	1	5	3
5	3	1	4	2	6
1	6	5	3	4	2
2	4	3	5	6	1
6	1	4	2	3	5
3	5	2	6	1	4

Page 26-27

Wordsearches

```
c i t y b r e a k r
c r o i s s a n t t
w i n d m i l l s o
k s a g f i c i e u
g h i s t o r y j r
k d m p i z z a c i
p a e l l a s h o s
r n e v y t p r p t
a c c o r d i o n s
a e f l a m e n c o
```

```
g i p z c p c r t k
a a o e z h j m s i
c j e g r e e c e r
a g v o e a t g n e
s c f r a n c e g l
p l u a p r l r l a
a y w a l e s m a n
i x s c o t l a n d
n s s w e d e n d r
z l o i t a l y e r
```

Spot the difference

Page 28–29

Guess what?

Page 30–31

1) b – Pisa
2) c – The Netherlands
3) c – Eiffel
4) b – Paella
5) b – Croissant
6) a – Vienna
7) b – Lake Bled
8) b – Spain
9) a – The Alps
10) a – Denmark

Maze

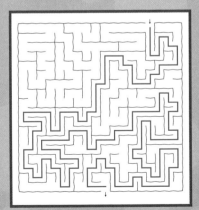

Word wheels

Netherlands, France

Solutions

Crosswords

```
R E L I A B L E
    A   V       V
B A R   A R E A S
    G   L       D
E Y E L A S H E S
  E       N   O
B A S I C     R E D
  R       H   S
  S E V E R E L Y
```

Keyword: GHANA

```
C U C U M B E R
    A   Y       U
F A R   S E E M S
    D   T       B
F I S H E R M A N
  S       R   U
B A M B I     M U D
  A       E
C O N S T A N T
```

Keyword: SUDAN

Sudokus

3	6	5	1	2	4
1	2	4	5	3	6
6	1	2	3	4	5
4	5	3	2	6	1
5	3	6	4	1	2
2	4	1	6	5	3

2	3	4	6	1	5
6	5	1	3	2	4
4	1	5	2	6	3
3	6	2	5	4	1
1	2	3	4	5	6
5	4	6	1	3	2

6	2	3	1	5	4
5	1	4	2	3	6
3	4	2	5	6	1
1	5	6	3	4	2
4	3	1	6	2	5
2	6	5	4	1	3

Wordsearches

```
c p y r a m i d s r
o r m a v d u b h k
f b c i a e r r s p
f t a n s s j d a h
e w s f a e s u v y
e s s o f r p a a e
w m a r a t h o n n
i e v e r p i a n a
c l a s i o n p a x
f h s t a y x s y p
```

```
f g u i n e a p s s
l a g l t g a n t n
z m o g h a n a u t
o o k e y z i f n u
e r e o e e l a i r
i o n t n l e r s o
i c y j a l z m i p
p c a l g e r i a r
m o u n t a i n s n
l l x o z a e g z m
```

94

Close Up

1 – 4 Giraffe
2 – 3 Lion
3 – 5 Elephant
4 – 2 Gorilla
5 – 6 Camel
6 – 1 Hippo

Guess what?

1) c – Bunny chow
2) a – River Nile
3) b – Sahara
4) b – Morocco
5) c – Cedi
6) a – Cairo
7) c – Lagos
8) a – Asia
9) b – Kenya
10) a – Safari

Maze

Word wheels

Egypt, Ethiopia

Solutions

Crosswords

```
D I S A S T E R   R
    T   P       A
B E E   E A S T
    A   C
A R M S T R O N G
  A     A   P
U P S E T     E E L
  I     O   R
  D E C R E A S E
```

Keyword: NEPAL

```
  T H R O U G H
S   U     R   S
P E R M A N E N T
I   R   C   E   A
D   I   T   T   B
E   C   O   I   L
R E A R R A N G E
S   N       G   S
  W E A K E S T
```

Keyword: KUWAIT

Sudokus

1	5	3	2	4	6
6	4	2	3	5	1
4	3	1	5	6	2
5	2	6	1	3	4
2	6	5	4	1	3
3	1	4	6	2	5

4	3	2	5	6	1
1	6	5	2	3	4
5	4	3	1	2	6
2	1	6	4	5	3
3	2	4	6	1	5
6	5	1	3	4	2

4	5	3	1	2	6
2	6	1	3	5	4
1	4	5	6	3	2
3	2	6	5	4	1
5	1	4	2	6	3
6	3	2	4	1	5

Wordsearches

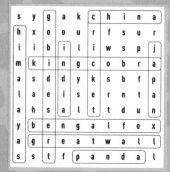

```
s y g a k c h i n a
h x o o u r f s u r
i i b i l i w s p j
m k i n g c o b r a
a s d d y k s b f p
l a e i s e r n t a
a h s a l t t d u n
y b e n g a l f o x
a g r e a t w a l l
s s t f p a n d a l
```

```
g g b a m b o o w g
r t p a k i s t a n
a x e w s u a u s a
s o u t h k o r e a
s t h o n g k o n g
l t h a i l a n d s
a p q j u d o n v i
n s e z o r e l m l
d r t i g e r t o k
s i n g a p o r e m
```

Spot the difference

Page 52–53

Page 54–55

Guess what?

1) b – 4.5 billion
2) c – New Delhi
3) b – Green
4) a – Chicken satay
5) a – Mount Everest
6) c – Java
7) a – The Great Wall of China
8) b – Red and white
9) b – Tokyo
10) a – Bangkok

Maze

Word wheels

China, Malaysia

Solutions

Page
58–59

Crosswords

Crossword 1 grid:
```
V   H   T
DIFFICULT
 E  B  R   I
TWO ENTER
O   R  L   E
TRAIN END
A   N  O
LIGHTNING
    E  E   E
```

Keyword: HAWAII

Crossword 2 grid:
```
I   S       T
AMOUNT  E   E
M   I  ROLL
E   TIE    E
IDEA    ALSO
I   BUS    C
NAIL    U  O
T   EUROPE
E       E   E
```

Keyword: CANADA

Page
60–61

Sudokus

Sudoku 1:
3	6	1	2	5	4
2	5	4	3	1	6
4	2	6	1	3	5
1	3	5	4	6	2
6	4	3	5	2	1
5	1	2	6	4	3

Sudoku 2:
5	3	2	4	6	1
1	4	6	3	5	2
6	5	3	1	2	4
2	1	4	5	3	6
4	2	5	6	1	3
3	6	1	2	4	5

Sudoku 3:
5	6	3	4	1	2
4	1	2	5	6	3
1	4	5	2	3	6
3	2	6	1	4	5
2	3	4	6	5	1
6	5	1	3	2	4

Page
62–63

Wordsearches

Wordsearch 1:
```
s g r w b t b l m s
z c a n a d a i e k
b n c b s s l c x y
v e n a k t d i i s
e w t k e r e h o c
s y o e t g a c o r
a o w b b f g y y a
r r e a s f o o o p
s k r l l l h c t e
x s s l l i n y e r
```

Wordsearch 2:
```
l a k e h u r o n l
h o l l y w o o d o
c h i c a g o l p s
p i m f l o r i d a
t o r o n t o y f n
o r u a t n l i u g
a i t s e a t t l e
k v v d t k s v d l
k e y l i m e p i e
y r u a s t e x a s
```

98

Spot the difference

Page 64–65

Guess what?

Page 66–67

1) b – English, Spanish and French

2) a – Washington, D.C.

3) b – Toronto

4) b – Canada

5) a – Purple

6) b – Key lime pie

7) b – Bread

8) b – Peso

9) c – Ottawa

10) a – California

Maze

Word wheels

Jamaica, Mexico

Solutions

Crosswords

Crossword 1

T	W	E	L	V	E					
E		I			S				T	
E		G	O	T		T	O	E	N	
N		H		O			R		A	
A	S	T	R	O	N	A	U	T	C	
G		E		T			I		A	
E	Y	E		H	U	G			C	
R		N		H					L	
			C	E	N	T	R	E		

Keyword: CHILE

Crossword 2

T	R	A	V	E	L					
O		N			I			I		E
R		Y	E	S		R	U	N		N
T		T		Y		R		V		
O	T	H	E	R	W	I	S	E		
I		I		U		T		L		O
S	U	N		P	E	A				P
E		G				T				E
			F	R	E	E	Z	E		

Keyword: ARGENTINA

Sudokus

Sudoku 1

3	4	6	2	5	1
2	5	1	3	6	4
1	6	2	5	4	3
4	3	5	1	2	6
5	1	4	6	3	2
6	2	3	4	1	5

Sudoku 2

4	2	1	6	3	5
3	5	6	4	1	2
1	6	4	2	5	3
5	3	2	1	6	4
2	1	3	5	4	6
6	4	5	3	2	1

Sudoku 3

6	2	3	4	1	5
5	1	4	2	3	6
4	6	2	3	5	1
3	5	1	6	4	2
2	3	5	1	6	4
1	4	6	5	2	3

Wordsearches

Wordsearch 1

c	k	s	p	s	w	c	p	l	a
a	m	a	c	a	w	h	o	i	b
r	i	m	l	o	t	o	s	r	i
n	a	b	i	p	m	c	o	a	s
i	u	a	m	a	z	o	n	z	s
v	r	a	a	u	u	l	g	i	r
a	n	g	e	l	f	a	l	l	s
l	u	t	x	o	t	t	q	s	y
s	m	c	o	f	f	e	e	b	a
u	u	e	a	y	t	n	h	a	v

Wordsearch 2

m	v	u	v	a	o	b	e	e	t
z	p	r	e	c	p	o	q	c	u
j	i	u	n	o	e	l	n	u	v
a	r	g	e	n	t	i	n	a	f
g	a	u	z	c	p	v	t	d	t
u	n	a	u	a	e	i	g	o	u
n	h	y	e	u	r	a	j	r	r
r	a	p	l	a	t	a	u	w	t
d	s	t	a	a	c	h	i	l	e
s	o	o	t	h	c	g	a	q	p

Spot the difference

Guess what?

1) b – Sugar Loaf Mountain
2) a – Peru
3) c – Chile
4) b – Beef
5) b – Paraguay
6) a – Yellow, blue and red
7) c – Amazon
8) a – Aconcagua
9) c – Suriname
10) a – Portuguese

Maze

Word wheels

Argentina, Brazil

Solutions

Page 82–83

Crosswords

Crossword 1:

T	I	G	E	R	S		
O		R	O		M		W
B	O	A	R	D	G	A	M	E
O		F			G		E
G	I	F	T		B	A	C	K
G		I			Z		E
A	T	T	E	N	T	I	O	N
N		I		U		N		D
			A	N	G	E	L	S

Keyword: KANGAROO

Crossword 2:

R	A	I	L	W	A	Y		V
E				H		I		O
N		G		I	D	E	A	L
E		Y		R		L		U
W	I	M	B	L	E	D	O	N
A		N		P		E		T
B	E	A	N	O		D		A
L		S		O				R
E		T	O	L	S	T	O	Y

Keyword: AUSTRALIA

Page 84–85

Sudokus

Sudoku 1:

3	1	2	5	6	4
4	6	5	2	3	1
6	4	3	1	5	2
5	2	1	3	4	6
2	3	6	4	1	5
1	5	4	6	2	3

Sudoku 2:

5	3	2	6	4	1
1	4	6	3	5	2
6	2	3	5	1	4
4	5	1	2	3	6
3	6	4	1	2	5
2	1	5	4	6	3

Sudoku 3:

4	5	2	3	6	1
6	1	3	2	4	5
5	2	1	6	3	4
3	4	6	1	5	2
2	6	4	5	1	3
1	3	5	4	2	6

Page 86–87

Wordsearches

Wordsearch 1:

k	a	u	s	t	r	a	l	i	a
a	l	r	o	h	s	r	e	k	v
n	e	w	z	e	a	l	a	n	d
g	a	x	f	o	r	t	a	s	x
a	w	p	s	u	r	f	i	n	g
r	p	e	r	t	h	e	d	a	r
o	w	o	m	b	a	t	i	r	f
o	p	e	r	a	h	o	u	s	e
r	q	p	a	c	i	f	i	c	h
i	p	e	l	k	o	a	l	a	i

Wordsearch 2:

a	w	b	a	r	b	e	c	u	e
v	e	g	e	m	i	t	e	g	a
s	l	a	d	e	l	a	i	d	e
y	l	w	w	a	l	l	a	b	y
d	i	d	g	e	r	i	d	o	o
n	n	c	a	n	b	e	r	r	a
e	g	o	l	d	c	o	a	s	t
y	t	r	n	y	s	r	i	p	k
b	o	n	d	i	b	e	a	c	h
s	n	r	w	h	s	r	s	w	n